THRILLING ADVENTURES

OF THE

WHALER ALCYONE

KILLING MAN-EATING SHARKS
IN THE INDIAN OCEAN
HUNTING KANGAROOS
IN AUSTRALIA

∴

Ten Illustrations

GEORGE BARKER, PUBLISHER

PEABODY, MASS.

1916

Copyright, 1916, by GEORGE BARKER

THE TUDOR PRESS
BOSTON

GEORGE BARKER

AUTHOR'S NOTE

Crowded with adventure, the boyhood and young manhood of George Barker, a musical instructor and a former member of the Boston police force, make a remarkable story.

At the age of twelve he roamed across the United States. He had hundreds of decidedly sensational experiences. He narrowly escaped death from sharks while whaling in the Indian Ocean. In Australia he hunted kangaroos. His love for music finally led him to a place among prominent instructors. Every boy who appreciates a good thrilling story of adventure will enjoy this one of Mr. Barker's life.   THE AUTHOR.

CONTENTS

CONTENTS — *(Continued)*

ILLUSTRATIONS BY HERMAN POPP
BOSTON, MASS.

PART FIRST

EARLY LIFE OF GEORGE BARKER

MR. BARKER was born in 1852
on Warren Street, Boston, son
of Thomas Taft Barker, a native of
Nottingham, England, and Jane Lor-
raine, the eldest daughter of Ben-
jamin and Abbey Fuller, of Dorchester,
Mass.

In the Barker family there were six
children, three boys and three girls;
George being the youngest.

At the age of six years his family
moved to New York, his father at that
time being engaged in the manufacture

of laces was obliged to move his business to the seat of activity. Shortly after their arrival in New York George was sent to visit an old friend of the family, a retired clergyman then living in Beloit, Wis.

ACROSS THE CONTINENT

A stay of a few weeks there fully satisfied the desires for this vacation and George began to long for home. It was here that the travels and adventures of this young man began. His parents preferring that he stay there a while longer made no preparations for a return trip, so George was obliged to think of some means of getting home. The only method open was to walk, and to walk George started.

After a long and tiresome journey he arrived in Chicago, Ill., where, becoming tired of a trip of this kind, he secured a

11

berth as cabinboy on a schooner bound for Buffalo, N. Y., by way of Lakes Michigan and Erie.

From Buffalo he worked his way to Albany, principally by driving a mule team on the Erie Canal.

A raft going down the Hudson furnnished his passage from that city to New York, so that he had completed a trip of several hundred miles without the expenditure of a cent.

Shortly after his arrival in New York City he was taken back to Boston, and at the age of fifteen years secured a position as office boy in Henry Tolman's music store on Washington Street, near Temple Place. His family still being in New York, he obtained board with a family by the name of Norton, living on Bedford Street. In this family were two daughters; the younger, Lillian, afterward became famous as an operatic star, and under the name of Madame Nordica she was familiar to all theatre goers, and is now missed by many from the program.

AWAY AGAIN

In the fall of 1869, not being content with the prospects of an office boy in a music store, George, at the age of sixteen, shipped on the *Alcyone*, a whaler of ninety-two tons, bound for the Indian Ocean, carrying a crew of twenty-three men and boys. This trip is considered the most exciting of his life.

The first day out the whaler encountered very heavy weather. Most of the boys were seasick, George included. They were so ill they could hardly eat the coarse food served, and longed for home. Some of the boys stole the pots and ket-

14

tles from the galley and threw them overboard, thinking that the loss of them
would cause the captain to turn back to
port and they would have a chance to
escape. The captain, however, did not
consider the loss of a few kettles sufficient
reason for turning back, so the vessel
continued on her course. Such cooking
utensils as were needed were picked up
from other vessels at sea.

For this trick the boys were put on a
short allowance, and their lives were
made miserable during the rest of the
voyage.

Hard-tack and tough salt meat com-

15

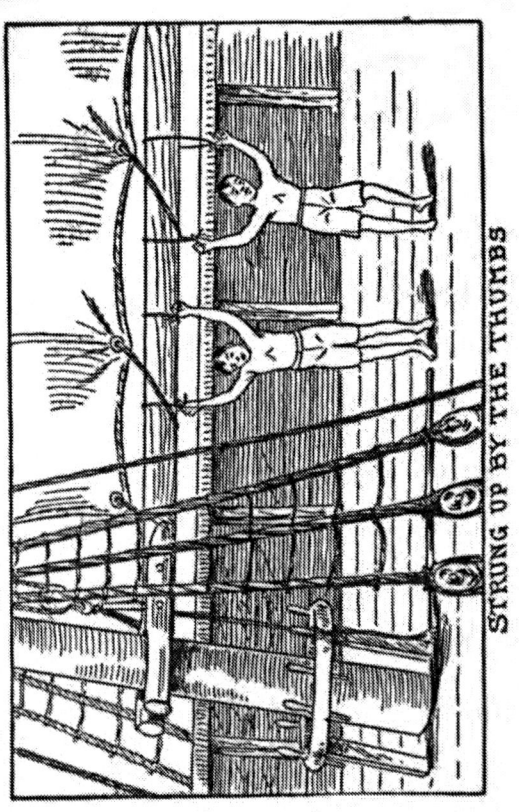

STRUNG UP BY THE THUMBS

16

prised the bulk of their daily meals, it being necessary to bake the former in a hot oven before rendering it safe to eat. Occasionally, this diet was varied by flying fish that were caught on the deck. These fish are similar to our smelts in size and taste. The flying fish were attracted by a lantern hung over the side of the rigging. They would fly on board in large schools; the crew gathered nearly two hundred of these fish in one school.

Another form of punishment was hanging up by the thumbs. The boys were hung by the thumbs and made to stand on their toes for two hours at a

GETTING THE ROPES END

time. This punishment was frightful, the rolling of the schooner adding to the misery of the culprit, and the after-effects being even worse.

Orders were given with a rope's end laid across their backs. No attempt was made to gain the good-will of the boys; they were treated as slaves.

On one occasion a large number of sea-gulls and albatross, acting as though they were crazy, turning somersaults and flapping their wings on the surface of the ocean, followed in the wake of the ship.

Upon investigation it was learned that these birds were in spasms from gorging themselves with whale meat from the carcass of a dead whale.

After cruising about the South Atlantic for eleven months, out of sight of land, the coast of Africa was sighted. The *Alcyone* rounded the Cape of Good Hope and sailed up through the Mozambique Channel, between the coast of Africa and the Island of Madagascar, entering the Bay of Tullear.

Nearing the shore, the vessel was surrounded by the natives, who swam out carrying cocoanuts and bananas under one arm and swimming with the other. The king of the tribe paddled out to the boat in a canoe. He was a comical old fellow, wearing a military hat and overcoat, which were the extent of his dress. He tried to explain to the crew that he was there for the purpose of collecting port charges.

A live steer, a pig and a coop of hens were taken on board, which the captain paid for with two rolls of highly-colored cotton cloth. The steer ran wild as soon as the whaler struck rough water and chased the sailors from the wheel. The captain shot the steer. The crew then had a feast of fresh meat, the first since they left America. The hencoop broke

21

loose and the hens flew overboard. The Portuguese cook burned to a crisp the pig which was to have been served for a Christmas dinner.

After leaving this port the whaler was headed for the Indian Ocean. It stopped on the way at Bird Island.

As the shore of this island was neared, hundreds of sea-gulls flew into the air. Some of the boys went ashore in a small boat and looked the island over. Quantities of large red bananas were growing there; these afforded the boys a feast. There were a number of giant sea-turtles sunning themselves on the shore. They turned two of the larger ones over on their backs and later towed them to the schooner. The next day turtle soup was served for dinner.

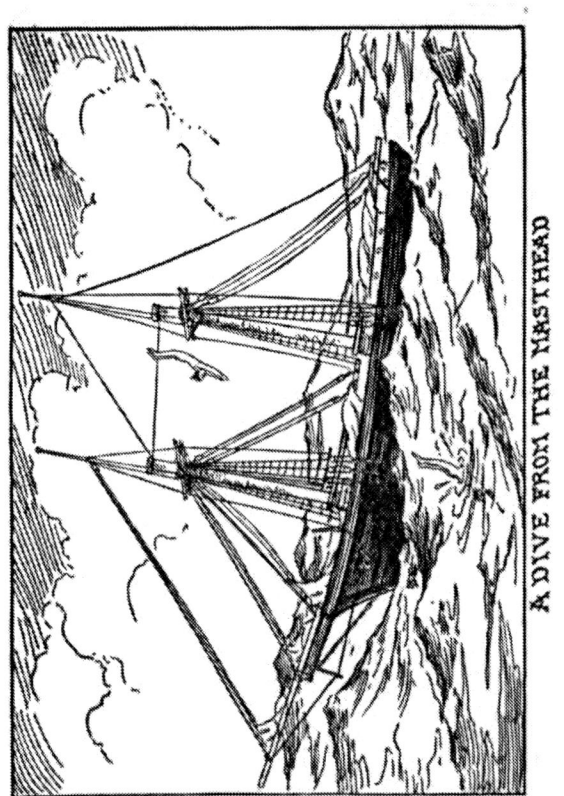

A DIVE FROM THE MASTHEAD

SWIMMING IN THE OCEAN

A hurricane in the Indian Ocean was a frequent occurrence. The sea was lashed into waves which rolled mountain high, but the *Alcyone* was built for a pilot boat and stood all kinds of rough weather. After these storms had subsided, there would scarcely be a breath of air stirring. On these occasions the boys would strip off their shirts and pants and plunge into the warm sea. One of the sailors, being an expert swimmer, frequently made a dive from the masthead, and as the *Alcyone* rolled to leeward he would dive off into space. When the vessel was on the crest of a mountain wave the swimmers were in a valley.

The lookout at the fore-topmast watched out for sharks. When he saw the dark shadow of a shark in the sea, he would shout to the boys, and they would scramble on board.

TOWED BY A WHALE

While cruising about the Indian Ocean the first sperm whale was sighted, attention being called to this fact by the man in the lookout shouting, "There she blows." Boats were immediately lowered and pulled out to a large school of whales. When within about a hundred yards of them the sailors shipped their oars and took the paddles, so as to make as little noise as possible. They made for one exceptionally large one that appeared not to be aware of their presence, and when within about ten yards of it the boat-steerer drove the harpoon into it. As

27

Towed by a Whale

soon as hit, the whale turned flukes and started for the bottom. There was plenty of rope attached to the harpoon which was let out. It soon came up and started along the surface of the water at a rate close to twenty miles an hour, towing the boat along with it.

It kept this pace up for some time, but after a while became tired out. The boat then drew up to him and the captain drove a lance through its heart, putting an end to the racing. The modern method of capturing whales is to shoot a vial of cyanide of potassium into the whale with a bomb which explodes inside the whale, killing it instantly.

29

The boat was towed out of sight of
the *Alcyone*. After having been towed
about twenty-five miles they ran short of
food and fresh water. Nevertheless, they
pulled the boat with their eighteen-foot
oars for several hours. A breeze sprung
up and the schooner sailed to their relief.
They then fastened a rope to the whale's
flukes (tail). Another rope was passed
through the whale's head and made fast
to the stern of the schooner on the weather
side. But this job was not very success-
fully done, and the whale started to drift
away from the side of the schooner, there-
by starting, though he did not know it at

30

the time, one of the most thrilling experiences of Mr. Barker's reminiscences.

As soon as the captain became aware
that his catch was not secured, he offered
a pound of tobacco to the sailor who would
go over on the whale and make fast the
rope. Mr. Barker offered to do the job,
not realizing the danger and not noticing
that no other man on board was ready to
accept this offer, acceptable as a quantity
of tobacco was at that time.

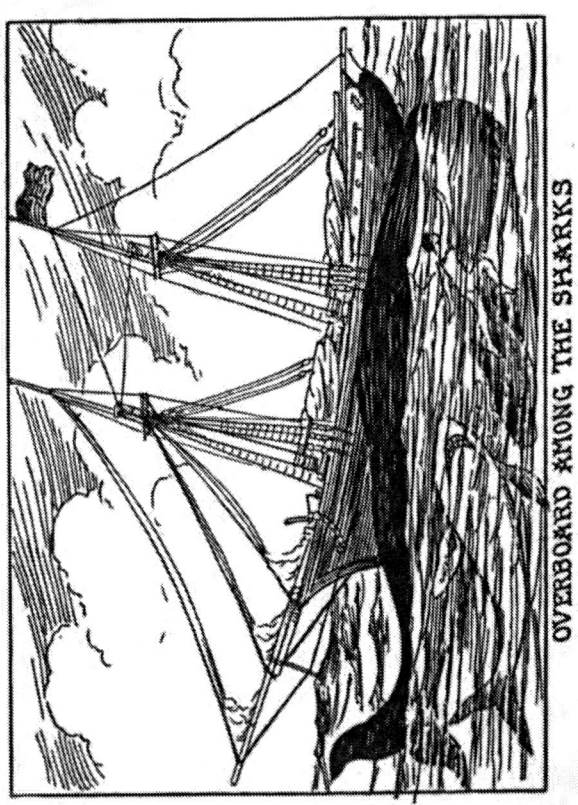

OVERBOARD AMONG THE SHARKS

OVERBOARD AMONG THE SHARKS

The mate tied a rope under his arms and he jumped into the sea and slipped down between the whale and the side of the schooner and worked his way along until he came to the head. Fastening the rope securely, he shouted to the boys on deck to haul him up.

When near the deck of the vessel he noticed that one of the crew was standing on a staging with a long lance in his hand, while another held a lantern, and all wore a scared look on their faces. Upon landing on the deck he asked the meaning of this, and was told that the water around

33

the whale's body was filled with sharks and that several times the lances were thrown close to him to ward off these man-eating monsters.

He then looked over the side of the schooner and by the aid of the lantern could see several sharks swimming about. He was then convinced that the officers of a whaler cared but little for a man's or a boy's life. Nothing further was done that night.

CUTTING OFF THE BLUBBER

In the morning the cutting-up process was actually started.

Two men went over on the staging, which was lowered from the side of the whaler to just above the whale's body, and with a long, sharp lance cut the blubber down the sides into strips about two feet wide. As fast as one of the strips was cut a large hook on a tackle was made fast to it and it was hauled aboard. According to the custom the whale blubber was then lowered to the deck, cut into small pieces and tried out in a swinging caldron. A wood fire being started the scraps of the

35

CUTTING OFF THE BLUBBER

blubber were used for fuel, which made a hot fire.

An idea of the size of this capture can be had from the fact that ninety barrels of oil were taken from it, ten barrels of clear sperm oil having been taken out of the head alone.

When a whale was captured the cook fried doughnuts in the hot froth of the whale's oil and these were looked upon as a delicacy.

One barrel of sperm oil is valued at sixty dollars. The crew worked on shares and each got one barrel out of one hundred and seventy-five barrels (or on 175th lay).

37

AMBERGRIS

When a whale is sick it falls behind, being unable to keep up with the school. Ambergris is undigested food of a sick whale. It is worth its weight in gold. It is used by manufacturers of perfume. The Mohammedans burn it in their churches.

CATCHING BLACKFISH

When a school of blackfish was sighted all three boats were lowered into the sea. Each boat was furnished with harpoons attached to large buckets with a rope. When a boat got in among the school of blackfish one of the officers drove the harpoons into them, the bucket, acting as a drag, retarded the speed of the fish. The boat easily kept pace, while the officers drove the lance into them. The best kind of a drag is a six-foot plank attached to the harpoon with a rope in such a manner that the strain of the rope drags the plank broadside through the water.

39

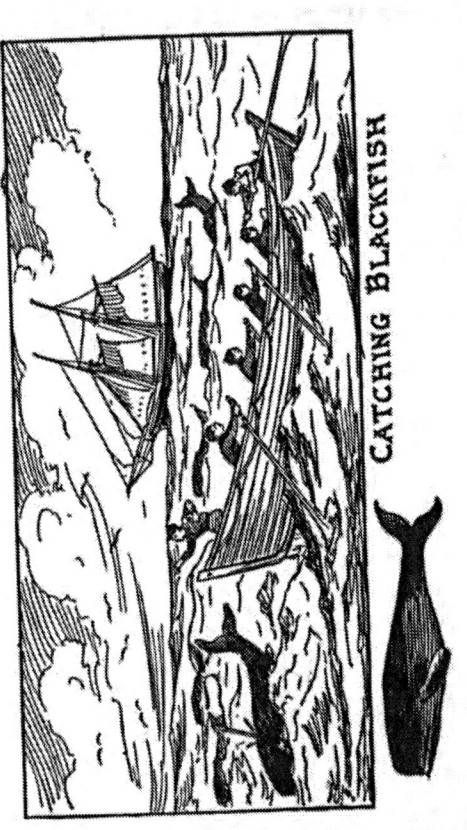

CATCHING BLACKFISH

40

The boys often trowled a piece of whale meat attached to a line from the stern of the schooner. Whenever a shark came within range they would drive a sharp lance into its body. Sometimes the lance would be driven clear through the body of the shark, but it would continue to fight for the whale meat. When the shark is struck in the back of the neck it dies instantly. As the dead shark sinks to the bottom of the ocean the other man-eating monsters follow and make a meal of him. Sometimes a man falls overboard and fights a shark with a sheath knife, the contest, lasting only a few seconds, ends in favor of the shark.

41

VISITING ROYALTY

Leaving this island, the mountainous Island of Mahee was sighted and the boat headed that way. They sailed as close to shore as they thought wise and then came to anchor. A few put off for shore in the tender and when they landed were greeted by as ugly a collection of human beings as was ever gotten together. These people were little short of savages, and had it not been for the fact that their "king" was a white man who had complete control of his subjects, the visit might have resulted disastrously. They were invited ashore by "His Ma-

42

jesty" and royally entertained. He informed them that he had been a mate on a vessel which was wrecked in the vicinity of the island and had managed to reach shore. Instead of meeting the fate of most sailors cast upon barbarous islands, he was warmly greeted by the natives, especially the women, and after a feast and other official ceremonies, which consisted largely of a rough and tumble fight, he was crowned king, the crown consisting of an American-made hat, originally belonging to some less fortunate shipwrecked sailor.

Despite all this glory, being king of a

lot of uncivilized beings did not appeal to him and he begged the captain to allow him to escape on his vessel, so he could return to civilization. The captain, however, was afraid to undertake such a move, fearing the natives would learn of it before he got away and make an attack. From the actions of certain of the tribe, it was thought they mistrusted some such movement and the visit was brought to a close, anchor being weighed next morning. The last seen of the "king" he was standing on shore watching with longing glances the departure of the boat.

CATCHING PORPOISES

Leaving the Island of Mahee, attention was turned to catching porpoises
and this proved to be the only real sport
on the trip. It was not long before they
ran into a school. The porpoise is a
specie of whale, and when fully grown will
weigh about three hundred pounds. They
sometimes follow a vessel for miles. As
these appeared to be exceptionally large
ones, the captain ordered a man out on
the martingale under the bowsprit. He
had a harpoon similar to that used in
spearing whales, to which was attached a
long rope.

45

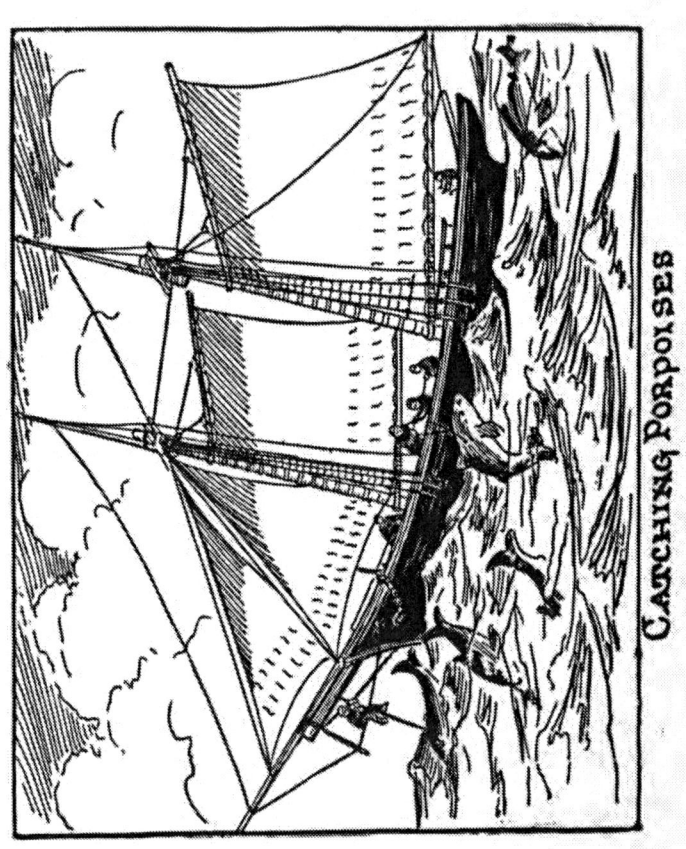

CATCHING PORPOISES

When the harpoon is driven into the body of the porpoise, the strain on the rope which is fastened to the fore-rigging unlocks the head of the harpoon and forms a letter "T" inside the porpoise.

When a porpoise came under the bow he drove the harpoon into it and the men back on deck hauled it aboard. Sometimes they came faster than they could be hauled aboard and while swimming about the side of the schooner they went through all sorts of antics, sometimes jumping entirely out of the water. At night their presence was detected by a

47

streak of phosphorus which follows them, but it took considerable practice to hit one after dark. Aside from the fun of catching them, they served as an addition to the menu. The cook cut out the loins and after being mixed with salt pork, they were fried in the form of meat balls. The oil was extracted from the jaw and proved quite valuable, as it is used by jewelers for oiling watches.

Shortly after this, while cruising near the coast of the island, they ran aground on a coral reef, they being numerous in the vicinity, and damaged the bottom of the vessel quite seriously, so that the captain

48

was obliged to make for a civilized port for repairs. He headed for Mauritius, an island on the east coast of Madagascar, this being the nearest port, and the vessel was dry-docked.

This was just the opportunity the boys were looking for, and it did not take them long to get together what few things they had and leave the ship.

George and another lad with whom he had bunked started ashore just after dark. They met a negro named Johnson, who informed them that he kept a sailors' boarding-house. He offered to hide them away until the whaler sailed, saying that

49

they could pay him for his services out of their advanced money. This offer they declined. Soon after they learned that the proprietor of the sailors' boarding-house had visited the *Alcyone* and induced the crew to desert. He offered them the same inducement that he had previously offered George and his chum. The next day the captain of the whaler offered a reward of five dollars for each one of the deserters. Johnson notified the captain where to find his crew and received the reward.

Later in the evening they met the first mate of the *Robert Passenger*, a full-rigged ship bound for Melbourne, Australia, with a cargo of sugar. He said his crew was short-handed and offered to take them along.

At midnight George and his chum swam out to the *Robert Passenger*, which was to sail next morning. They climbed up on the martingale under the bow and went below through the forecastle. The following morning they were taken before the captain, who appeared to be surprised at their presence aboard the ship. He said that he could not turn back, but would turn them over to the British Consul when the ship arrived in port.

They cared but little what he did as long as they were away from the whaler, for by that time they were tired of whaling experiences.

This voyage, while decidedly more pleasant than the one just abandoned, was not at all cheerful. Hard work was laid out for them and they were kept at it.

One day while aloft sewing a patch on the mizzen-topstaysail the foot-rope broke and George fell to the deck, fully twenty feet below. His fall was broken to some extent by ropes, but he landed heavily on his back and felt the effects for some time after. This voyage lasted about thirty days.

Landing in Melbourne they found themselves thirteen thousand miles from home. Shortly after the captain summoned George and his chum to his cabin. They expected to be given up to the British Consul, but instead, to their great surprise, he handed each of them twenty dollars in gold. His chum was so impressed by the captain's generosity that he reshipped. George decided to remain in Australia.

From Melbourne he wandered out among the sheep ranches and finally secured employment branding sheep on one. Australia is the greatest sheep-

53

raising country in the world on account of the extremely warm climate. There is no snow or ice, but grass the year round.

Mr. Barker was employed on a sheep ranch of one hundred and seventy-five thousand sheep. Some of the shearers were experts. One old-timer had a record of shearing one hundred and five sheep in one day. The Australian sheep shearers' method of shearing sheep is different than others. They stand the sheep erect on their haunches, begin at the left side of the neck of the sheep, then walk around, taking the fleece off in one piece.

In this country Mr. Barker learned that the sheep are tied down, which results in their kicking and squirming. Generally one person holds the sheep while another shears.

HUNTING THE KANGAROO

One Sunday, after George had been on the ranch a while, the foreman suggested a kangaroo hunt. Horses and dogs were rounded up and everything made ready for the start. This hunt proved very interesting and different from anything George had before attempted. The dogs were sent ahead to start out a kangaroo much the same as in a fox hunt, and soon had one on the run. The chase was continued until the kangaroo began to tire. Then it backed up against a tree and prepared to fight. It sat erect on its haunches and with its hind feet struck at

56

the dogs. This sort of boxing did not last long, for one of the men on horseback came up behind and attacked it with stirrup irons.

When a kangaroo is on the run it carries its body at an angle of forty-five degrees. Great speed is acquired by springing off its powerful tail. A sharp, pointed hoof, which is used for a weapon, grows at the point of its hind feet. When attacked, the kangaroo sits erect upon its haunches, springs at, and lacerates, its enemy with its sharp, horned hoofs. When feeding, the kangaroo rests upon its short forepaws. Its principal food is grass.

57

HUNTING THE KANGAROO.

When danger approaches, the female picks up her young with her forepaws and places them in her pouch, which is located on the front of her body. When on the run, the forepaws do not touch the ground.

The Laughing Jackass

THE BOOMERANG

While returning from the hunt the party ran across some laughing jackasses, a native bird of Australia, somewhat larger than our American pigeon. These birds are built very stocky and are the worst enemies of the snakes which inhabit that country. They watched two of them making an attack. First they flew down over it and one caught hold of its tail while the other caught hold of its head. Then they flew up into the air, a distance of about two hundred feet and dropped it to the ground. As soon as it landed, they caught it up again and

61

repeated the same performance. This procedure was kept up until the snake was dead, then it served for a meal.

The Aborigines of Australia are experts at throwing the boomerang. The natives seldom miss their mark. Should they miss the object, the boomerang returns to them in a graceful curve. They frequently bring down the kangaroo, also an emu, a large native bird, a species of the African ostrich, but not quite so large. These birds are fast runners.

THE SHIP "PHAROS"

By this time Mr. Barker's love for travel had begun to cool and he turned his mind to business, with the idea of staying in Melbourne.

Leaving the sheep ranch he secured a position in a wholesale grocery store in Melbourne, where he remained until 1872. One day while passing down Burke Street he noticed a bulletin in a newspaper office, stating that the city of Boston had been largely destroyed by conflagration. This turned his thoughts to home, and he made up his mind to

63

get there as soon as possible and look up his relatives.

The following morning Mr. Barker looked up a ship bound for America and took the train for the harbor. All freight is shipped up the Yarra Yarra River, which connects Melbourne (an inland city) with the harbor. His attention was attracted by a fine large American ship, named *The Pharos*, sailing under an East Boston captain named Collier.

Fate of the "Alcyone"

Letter From Fred Wilson

MARINES' HOME,

HONG KONG, CHINA,

May 30, 1871.

Dear Chummie:

Here I am once more on dry land. Arrived at Hong Kong after a long stormy passage, farther away from home than ever before. I am, like yourself, tired of sea life. My last trip on the *Robert Passenger* has cured me forever of the sea. The *Robert Passenger* was recently condemned. We stood at the pumps day and night. I never expected to see land again. I shall never forget our dear old friend, the ship, that rescued us from our life on board the *Alcyone*.

I was recently informed that the owners of the *Alcyone* had advertised for her, not having heard from her for a long time. I was told

that the *Alcyone* was in the possession of a
Malay pirate crew; that she robbed and sunk
every small trader that she met while cruising
in the China Sea; but, on account of her speed,
she always managed to escape from her pur-
suers.

Write soon and do not forget,

YOUR CHUM FRED.

The Pharos was bound for Sydney
with ballast to take a cargo of coal across
the Pacific Ocean to San Francisco, Cal.

To Mr. Barker's great surprise the
second mate turned out to be Willie
Adams, an old boyhood chum of his.
They attended the Berkeley Sunday
School years before. This building is at
the corner of Berkeley Street and Warren

66

Avenue, Boston, now a moving-picture theater.

Mr. Barker shipped as able seaman on *The Pharos* and soon arrived in Sydney.

After loading up with cargo of coal, they started across the Pacific Ocean. Half way across they encountered heavy weather; squalls and gales were frequent. One series of squalls struck the ship every few moments.

Mr. Barker was put in the first mate's watch. The captain and first mate did not agree.

During the voyage one of these squalls struck the ship and put her on her beams'

67

end. Mr. Barker was then at the helm.
The captain was in his berth, but the
lurching of the ship threw him out.
He rushed up on deck and knocked the
mate down for not clewing up the sails.
Mr. Barker was at the time unable to
bring the helm down, so the captain gave
him a hand at it and they soon brought
her up in the wind. The crew was
largely made up of Scandinavians, Poles,
Russians and Danes. They were an ugly
set to manage. The only way the second
mate could manage them was by using
brass knuckles. They were fifty-eight
days crossing the Pacific.

THE FIJI ISLANDS

These islands are located in the Pacific Ocean, about two thousand miles in an easterly direction from Australia. The natives of the Fiji Islands are expert swimmers; for a small coin they will swim in among a school of sharks and drive a sheath knife into a vital part, killing the man-eating monster instantly. On account of the natives' dark skin they are immune from attack from sharks, while a white man would have a small chance of escape. A shark will not attack anything black in the sea.

The following letter and article were kindly contributed by Mr. George W. Crossett.

———

CLEVELAND, OHIO,

August 10, 1916

MR. GEORGE BARKER,

Peabody, Mass.

My dear Sir:

In reply to your request, it gives me pleasure to submit a contribution to your book, telling of an adventure among the natives of the Fiji Islands, hoping that it may be of interest to the readers of your book, which I trust may have a large sale. I shall anticipate with much pleasure receiving a copy as soon as it is published.

Wishing you success in your undertaking, I am, my dear Sir, with kind regards,

Very sincerely yours,

GEORGE W. CROSSETT

A YANKEE BOY AT A CANNIBAL FEAST

In the year 1854 I shipped on board the *Barque Dragon* from Salem, Mass., for a voyage to the Fiji Islands, New South Wales, Philippines and China. We sailed the 22d day of February (Washington's Birthday), crossed the equator March 16th, and on the 19th of May sighted the Fiji Islands.

The joyful cry of "Land Ho!" as it rings out and is echoed from the mast-head is a welcome sound to the ears of the weary mariner who has been for weeks and months tossed on a restless sea.

71

We came to anchor in the harbor of Levuka, on the Island of Ovalu, which was to be our home for two years, while gathering a cargo of *beche de mer* for the Chinese market. The natives at this time were rank cannibals, and we often saw the light of their fires in the big cocoanut grove behind the town, where they were celebrating their heathen rites in roasting pigs, and the prisoners that they had taken in war.

As a boy I soon learned to speak the language, and spent many evenings in the house of the chief, who took a great fancy to me and tried to get me to run away from the ship and live with them, promising to build me a house and a new canoe, and give me fifteen hundred yams and two wives.

I had often felt a strong desire to attend one of their cannibal feasts, and one night, after they had had a fight with the natives of another island, during which they had taken three prisoners, we saw the light of their fires in the grove, and heard their shouts as they were dancing the war dance. I started for the grove, and scouted among the trees until I saw where the chief was sitting, and coming up behind him I said, "*Siandra tui,*

73

Levuka" (Good evening, Chief). He replied, "*Siandra go, Geody*" (Good evening, George), "*Lootu kin drecky*" (Sit down). "*Sar vere carma quego*" (Do you want to eat?) I said, "What have you?" and he replied, "*Sa lavu na borku, na eku*" (Plenty pork and fish). I said, "*Quiou sa carma vaka lili* (I will eat a little). He then sent one of the men to the ovens; he soon came back with two small packages wrapped up in green banana leaves and handed them to the chief, who passed them to me saying, "*Canu quego, sar ve naku*" (eat, it is good). The package felt warm and

74

smelled good and savory like roast pork, and it tasted good, too. I asked the chief how many men they had killed, and he said *"tolu"* (three). I then bit on the piece that was tough, and when I looked at it, it was black like beefsteak, and as there were no cattle in the islands, I knew in a minute that it was a piece of one of the men that they had killed in battle. I turned to the chief, and holding out a piece of meat said, *"Athaba na carngo?"* (What is that?) He said, *"Na borka sar ve naka carna"* (pork, good, eat it). I replied, *"Singi na borka, na bogola, sar thur"* (it is not

75

pork, but a piece of one of the prisoners," and I threw it on the ground. The chief laughed and said, "eat it, and bye and bye you be good Fiji man. I said, "*Singi serra!*" (No siree).

The natives kept up their cannibal orgies until near morning, when I went back to the ship and turned in.

Passage was soon engaged by Mr. Barker on a steamer bound for Aspinwall, crossing the Isthmus of Panama by rail. Arriving in Boston, he looked up his brother who was the proprietor of a yeast business at Boston Highlands. That evening the brothers called upon their mother who resided in a little cottage on Lamartine Street, Jamaica Plain. She was overjoyed to behold her son George again, the youngest member of the Barker family, whom she had not seen for six years. He made his home with his mother and provided for her during the remainder of her life.

THE BOSTON POLICE DEPART-
MENT

M R. BARKER was appointed a member of the Boston police department December 26, 1876, by Mayor Cobb. He was detailed to Division 13, Jamaica Plain. The following year he was transferred to Division 10, Roxbury Crossing, and given Route 4, the hardest one in the division. He passed the greater number of his short days prosecuting cases in court. His route adjoined those of ex-Superintendent William H. Pierce, Captain "Ned" Gaskin, Captain George Wescott and ex-Chief Inspector William B. Watts. The foregoing named were all patrolmen at that time. Mr. Pierce was superintendent of the police department for fifteen years. He is largely responsible for the Boston police department's high standard of efficiency.

Mr. Barker watched with interest the advancement of these four members of the department, especially that of Superintendent Pierce, from patrolman to sergeant, lieutenant, captain, deputy superintendent and, finally, superintendent of a police force that is second to none.

80

At the time of Mr. Pierce's retirement
from the department he was banqueted
by the superior officers, including Commissioner O'Meara. He was presented
with a valuable diamond pin by his
police associates.

In the year 1880 a liquor-license squad
was appointed by the police commissioners, with an office at police head-
quarters. The entire responsibility of
enforcing the liquor-license law was
practically taken out of the captain's
hands and turned over to the liquor
squad. All liquor license applications
were investigated by the new squad.

81

The liquor dealer applied for his license, and the squad, of which Mr. Barker was a member, made a report. If favorable, the commissioners granted a license. If the report were unfavorable, the applicant would see his wholesale dealer or brewer and have him intercede for him. Then the politician and *snide* lawyer reaped a harvest.

The fee for a first-class victualer's license at that time was one hundred and twenty-five dollars. The inn-holder's license, with a privilege to sell Sundays, was three hundred. To-day the fee for a victualer's license is eleven hundred dollars, a difference of nine hundred and seventy-five dollars. The inn-holder pays proportionally higher. To-day the liquor-license income to the city of Boston is one million dollars. In the early eighties somebody else besides the city of Boston secured a large proportion of this fund.

Mr. Barker was assigned to Division 7, covering the East Boston division and the islands of the Boston Harbor.

The officers had instructions from the police commissioners to use all alike and give the dealers a chance to make a living. One of the license commissioners, a rabid prohibitionist, frequently gave the squad a lecture. He instructed them to see that the liquor laws were enforced.

After a while Mr. Barker, profiting by these lectures, resolved to clean up his division. He took out thirteen search warrants and, with the assistance of several police officers in plain clothes from outside stations, he set watches and landed on the kitchen bar-rooms simultaneously. From the thirteen places raided he won convictions in twelve. The records of the East Boston Municipal Court will substantiate this statement.

Mr. Barker was transferred back to

Station 10. At that time he was informed by his captain, Hawley Folsom,
that one of the commissioners was after
Mr. Barker's scalp, and warned him to
be on his guard. A few days later Mr.
Barker read in a Boston paper that a
hearing was to be held by the committee
on cities as to the advisability of a metropolitan police.

At this hearing of the committee on
cities held at the State House, the advisability of establishing a metropolitan
police force for the city of Boston and its
suburbs was debated, and it was largely
through evidence which Mr. Barker was

able to lay before the committee at that hearing that action was finally taken which brought this force into reality. This bill met with considerable opposition, one of the chief opposers being Major Jones, a police commissioner.

Mr. Barker preferred charges to Mayor Samuel Green against Mr. Jones and the other members of the commission, showing where they had neglected to perform their duty in several instances, one of the principal cases cited being the sale of liquors to minors, where no steps had been taken by those commissioners, even after complaints, to stop it. After a careful investigation by Mayor Green, Mr. Jones and his associates were removed from office for the good of the service.

On March 4, 1882, Mr. Barker was discharged from the police department for appearing at the State House in support of this bill. An East Boston police officer was also transferred to Brighton. He had to move his family and take his children out of school for attempting to enforce the liquor laws. His case was similar to Mr. Barker's. They were punished for doing their duty.

During the latter part of the year 1881, while Mr. Barker was a member of the liquor squad, there was a German picnic held at Armory Grove, near the Boylston Station. In the afternoon a gang of Italians from the North End put in an appearance and soon started a fight. Mr. Barker happened to be on a train that pulled into the depot at that time, and noticed two Italians who had a German down and were kicking and pounding him. As Mr. Barker rushed to his assistance, a third Italian aimed a baseball bat at the back of Mr. Barker's head, but fortunately just then "Billie" Mullin, an ex-officer, came along and knocked the bat out of the Italian's hands, probably saving Mr. Barker's life. By this time a detail of policemen from Division 13 put in an appearance. They arrested the Italians, who, when searched at the police station, were found to have their pockets filled with rocks. The following morning they were all sentenced to the house of correction.

One of the state's witnesses testified that he and several others watched the day patrolman hiding behind a building, where he remained until the fight was over and the arrests made. This same day policeman is now drawing a pension of half pay from the City of Boston.

A noted criminal, who was recently given a long sentence in the State Prison, made this remark: "There are two cities where police officers don't stand in with crooks — Boston, Mass., and Omaha, Neb."

THE STUDY OF MUSIC

MR. BARKER, being musically in-
clined, his father, having been
an organist in a church in England as well as being a violinist of no
mean ability, it was not long before he
was able to play the guitar, the instrument of his choice, in such a way as to
attract the attention of intimate friends.
After hearing him play, many of his ac-
quaintances became imbued with the
idea that they would like to play some
instrument, and Mr. Barker was pre-
vailed upon to teach them what he knew.
Finding work of this sort very much to

his liking, he undertook the study of such musical instruments as the violin, mandolin and banjo, with the idea of teaching.

After having acquired the necessary instruction in this line, he opened a studio for the study of stringed instruments. At that time he had the distinction of being the only teacher of the mandolin in New England. This proved the most successful undertaking of his career up to this time, and it was not long before he had a large class of pupils. Being anxious to perpetuate his name along this, his chosen line, he undertook to compose simple pieces for his scholars.

This move was also successful, as the pupils took kindly to the idea of getting a new piece of music with each lesson without being obliged to pay for it, and it was not long before he was composing in addition to his teaching. Some of his pieces became instant hits and are popular to-day with mandolin and glee clubs.

In 1885, Mr. Barker organized a mandolin orchestra, consisting of mandolins, guitars, violins, flute, 'cello and harp, furnishing music for weddings, dinner parties, receptions for the élite of Boston, also the concert stage.

This brought Mr. Barker into an

entirely different atmosphere from his duties as police officer at Station 10. During his thirty years' experience as instructor of music, Mr. Barker had over two thousand pupils, including the five violin and mandolin schools, with an average of two hundred and fifty pupils in these schools. The Springfield School had three hundred and twenty-five pupils. The different schools were located in Boston, Springfield, Pittsfield, Waterbury and Salem. Among the two thousand pupils there were several hundred private scholars. He wrote the following letter to a newspaper:

" To the Man About Town:

William Cardinal O'Connell is an expert performer on the mandolin. His Eminence studied the mandolin with me in the year 1887 and recently informed me, while in Rome, as instructor at the American College, that his mandolin was a great source of pleasure to him and that he had never lost interest in this charming little instrument. Cardinal O'Connell is a fine musician. His compositions for the voice, organ and piano have a wide circulation.

"GEORGE BARKER."

"Salem, Jan. 31."

Mr. Barker has composed and arranged a large number of musical compositions for the stringed instruments, which are now in circulation throughout the United States and Canada.

95

In 1908 Mr. Barker made an extended trip South, visiting the large cities and towns, and while at Washington, D. C., through Senator W. Murray Crane, received an invitation to attend President Roosevelt's diplomatic reception. The printed invitation is among the many souvenirs of his travels.

After leaving Washington, Mr. Barker visited several cities and towns along the Indian River, Florida, Ormand Beach, St. Augustine, Rockledge, Daytona, Polatka and Palm Beach. Those who have traveled extensively consider Palm Beach the paradise of the world.

Mr. Barker arranged a series of four concerts. The first concert was given March 9, 1886, at the Y. M. C. A. Union on Boylston Street, Boston, one hundred of Mr. Barker's mandolin, guitar and banjo pupils taking part in this concert. It was the most successful of the four concerts. Mr. Barker's pupils sold out the entire house some time before the night of the affair.

The prizes for selling tickets were as follows: First prize, a seventy-five dollar mandolin; second, a twenty dollar guitar; third prize, a ten dollar banjo. In addition, ten per cent on all other tickets sold.

The fourth concert, given at Pitts-field, was also a success.

The expenses of the first concert were one hundred and twenty dollars; total receipts four hundred dollars.

In 1911 he opened the "Bostonia School of Music" at Salem, enrolling a very large class, the pupils taking up the study of practically all classes of stringed instruments. Not a few who received their instruction from him have made a reputation on the vaudeville stage, and when playing in this vicinity make it a point to pay him a visit at his studio.

MEMORIES OF CHILDHOOD

Words and Music by
GEORGE BARKER

Breinigsville, PA USA
19 August 2009

222622BV00003B/25/A